Enough Rope

Poems of 1926 by
Dorothy Parker

Illustrated by
Lisa Shea

~ v2a ~

The original book "Enough Rope" by Dorothy Parker was published in 1926. It became public domain in 2022.

The initial book states:

The verses in this book were first printed in *Life*, *Vanity Fair*, *The New Yorker*, and *The New York World*.

Kindle ASIN: B09PZCJW4X

Paperback ISBN: 9798798701117

Contents

Introduction 1

PART I 3

    Threnody 4

    The Small Hours 5

    The False Friends 6

    The Trifler 7

    A Very Short Song 8

    A Well-Worn Story 9

    Convalescent 10

    The Dark Girl's Rhyme 11

    Epitaph 13

    Light of Love 14

    Wail 15

    The Satin Dress 16

    Somebody's Song 17

    Anecdote 18

    Braggart 19

    Epitaph for a Darling Lady 20

To a Much Too Unfortunate Lady 21

Paths 22

Hearthside 23

Rainy Night 25

For a Sad Lady 27

Recurrence 28

Story of Mrs. W— 29

The Dramatists 30

August 31

The White Lady 32

I Know I Have Been Happiest 33

Testament 34

"I Shall Come Back" 35

Condolence 36

The Immortals 37

A Portrait 38

PART TWO 39

Portrait of the Artist 40

Chant for Dark Hours 41

Unfortunate Coincidence 42

Verse Reporting Late Arrival at a Conclusion.................... 43

Inventory 44

Now at Liberty 45

Comment.. 46

Plea.. 47

Pattern 48

De Profundis 49

They Part.. 50

Ballade of a Great Weariness................................... 51

L'ENVOI: 52

Résumé... 53

Renunciation 54

Day-Dreams 55

The Veteran.. 57

Prophetic Soul... 58

Verse for a Certain Dog 59

Folk Tune.. 60

Godspeed... 61

Song of Perfect Propriety 62

Social Note 64

One Perfect Rose 65

Ballade at Thirty-five 66

L'ENVOI: 67

The Thin Edge 68

Spring Song 69

Love Song 70

Indian Summer 71

Philosophy 72

For an Unknown Lady 73

The Leal 74

Finis 75

Words of Comfort to he Scratched on a Mirror 76

Men 77

News Item 78

Song of One of the Girls 79

Lullaby 80

Faut de Mieux 81

Roundel 82

A Certain Lady 83

Observation 84

Symptom Recital 85

Fighting Words 86

Rondeau Redouble 87

Autobiography 88

The Choice 89

Ballade of Big Plans 90

L'ENVOI: 91

General Review of the Sex Situation 92

Inscription for the Ceiling of a Bedroom 93

Pictures in the Smoke 94

Biographies 95

Nocturne 98

Interview 99

Song in a Minor Key 100

Experience 101

Neither Bloody Nor Bowed 102

The Burned Child.. 103

Summary 104

Dedication 107

About the Editor... 108

Free Ebooks 109

Introduction

Dorothy Parker was born on August 22nd, 1893. The world was changing immensely for women during this time period. Dorothy was there to witness and comment on it all.

While her family was fairly well off, Dorothy did not have an easy childhood. She grew up in the heart of New York City. Her mother died when she was five. Her father reportedly abused her, and she didn't get along with her stepmother. Her stepmother then died when she was nine. Dorothy was sent off to finishing school. By twenty her father was dead, too.

A fan of the arts. Dorothy turned to teaching piano and writing poetry to make some money. She quickly got jobs with Vogue and Vanity Fair. This was her true path to happiness. She became close friends with other writers and they would have lunch together at the Algonquin hotel. Their "Algonquin Round Table" featured a wide variety of writers, poets, and intellectuals.

Her fame grew, and she wrote poetry for a wide variety of magazines. She was on the founding board for The New Yorker in 1926. A year later, she published this book. It received great reviews.

Dorothy lived a long, productive life. She finally passed away at age 73 of a heart attack. She donated her estate to Martin Luther King's efforts. Her ashes were part of a memorial garden at the NAACP office. When the NAACP moved in 2020, the ashes were relocated to a family plot in the Bronx.

My proceeds from this book support local arts programs.

~ Lisa Shea

PART I

Threnody

Lilacs blossom just as sweet
Now my heart is shattered.
If I bowled it down the street.
Who's to say it mattered?
If there's one that rode away
What would I be missing?
Lips that taste of tears, they say.
Are the best for kissing.

Eyes that watch the morning star
Seem a little brighter;
Arms held out to darkness are
Usually whiter.
Shall I bar the strolling guest.
Bind my brow with willow.
When, they say, the empty breast
Is the softer pillow?

That a heart falls tinkling down.
Never think it ceases.
Every likely lad in town
Gathers up the pieces.
If there's one gone whistling by
Would I let it grieve me?
Let him wonder if I lie;
Let him half believe me.

The Small Hours

No more my little song comes back;
    And now of nights I lay
My head on down, to watch the black
    And wait the unfailing gray.

Oh, sad are winter nights, and slow;
    And sad's a song that's dumb;
And sad it is to lie and know
    Another dawn will come.

Dorothy Parker

The False Friends

They laid their hands upon my head
A They stroked my cheek and brow;
And time could heal a hurt, they said,
And time could dim a vow.

And they were pitiful and mild
Who whispered to me then,
"The heart that breaks in April, child,
Will mend in May again."

Oh, many a mended heart they knew.
So old they were, and wise.
And little did they have to do
To come to me with lies!

Who flings me silly talk of May
Shall meet a bitter soul;
For June was nearly spent away
Before my heart was whole.

The Trifler

Death's the lover that I'd be taking;
  Wild and fickle and fierce is he.
Small's his care if my heart be breaking—
  Gay young Death would have none of me.

Hear them clack of my haste to greet him!
  No one other my mouth had kissed.
I had dressed me in silk to meet him—
  False young Death would not hold the tryst.

Slow's the blood that was quick and stormy.
  Smooth and cold is the bridal bed;
I must wait till he whistles for me—
  Proud young Death would not turn his head.

I must wait till my breast is wilted,
  I must wait till my back is bowed,
I must rock in the corner, jilted,—
  Death went galloping down the road.

Gone's my heart with a trifling rover.
  Fine he was in the game he played—
Kissed, and promised, and threw me over.
  And rode away with a prettier maid.

Dorothy Parker

A Very Short Song

Once, when I was young and true.
    Someone left me sad—
Broke my brittle heart in two;
    And that is very bad.

Love is for unlucky folk,
    Love is but a curse.
Once there was a heart I broke;
    And that; I think, is worse.

A Well-Worn Story

In April, in April,
My one love came along.
And I ran the slope of my high hill
To follow a thread of song.

His eyes were hard as porphyry
With looking on cruel lands;
His voice went slipping over me
Like terrible silver hands.

Together we trod the secret lane
And walked the muttering town.
I wore my heart like a wet, red stain
On the breast of a velvet gown.

In April, in April,
My love went whistling by.
And I stumbled here to my high hill
Along the way of a lie.

Now what should I do in this place
But sit and count the chimes.
And splash cold water on my face
And spoil a page with rhymes?

Convalescent

How shall I wail, that wasn't meant for weeping
Love has run and left me, oh, what then?
Dream, then, I must, who never can be sleeping;
hat if I should meet Love, once again?

What if I met him, walking on the highway?
Let him see how lightly I should care.
He'd travel his way, I would follow my way;
Hum a little song, and pass him there.

What if at night, beneath a sky of ashes.
He should seek my doorstep, pale with need?
There could he lie, and dry would be my lashes;
Let him stop his noise, and let me read.

Oh, but I'm gay, that's better off without him;
Would he'd come and see me, laughing here.
Lord! Don't I know I'd have my arms about him,
Crying to him, "Oh, come in, my dear!"

The Dark Girl's Rhyme

Who was there had seen us
    Wouldn't bid him run?
Heavy lay between us
    All our sires had done.

There he was, a-springing
    Of a pious race—
Setting hags a-swinging
    In a market-place;

Sowing turnips over
    Where the poppies lay;
Looking past the clover.
    Adding up the hay;

Shouting through the Spring song.
    Clumping down the sod;
Toadying, in sing-song.
    To a crabbèd god.

There I was, that came of
    Folk of mud and flame—
I that had my name of
    Them without a name.

Up and down a mountain
    Streeled my silly stock;
Passing by a fountain.
    Wringing at a rock;

Devil-gotten sinners.
    Throwing back their heads;
Fiddling for their dinners.
    Kissing for their beds.

Not a one had seen us
    Wouldn't help him flee.
Angry ran between us
    Blood of him and me.

How shall I be mating
    Who have looked above—
Living for a hating.
    Dying of a love?

Epitaph

The first time I died, I walked my ways;
I followed the file of limping days.

I held me tall, with my head flung up.
But I dared not look on the new moon's cup.

I dared not look on the sweet young rain.
And between my ribs was a gleaming pain.

The next time I died, they laid me deep.
They spoke worn words to hallow my sleep.

They tossed me petals, they wreathed me fern.
They weighted me down with a marble urn.

And I lie here warm, and I lie here dry.
And watch the worms slip by, slip by.

Dorothy Parker

Light of Love

Joy stayed with me a night——
Young and free and fair——•
And in the morning light
He left me there.

Then Sorrow came to stay.
And lay upon my breast;
He walked with me in the day.
And knew me best.

I'll never be a bride.
Nor yet celibate.
So I'm living now with Pride—
A cold bedmate.

He must not hear nor see.
Nor could he forgive
That Sorrow still visits me
Each day I live.

Wail

Love has gone a-rocketing,
    That is not the worst;
I could do without the thing.
    And not be the first.

Joy has gone the way it came.
    That is nothing new;
I could get along the same,—
    Many people do.

Dig for me the narrow bed.
    Now I am bereft.
All my pretty hates are dead,
    And what have I left?

The Satin Dress

Needle, needle, dip and dart,
Thrusting up and down.
Where's the man could ease a heart
Like a satin gown?

See the stitches curve and crawl
Round the cunning seams—
Patterns thin and sweet and small
As a lady's dreams.

Wantons go in bright brocades;
Brides in organdie;
Gingham's for the plighted maid;
Satin's for the free!

Wool's to line a miser's chest;
Crape's to calm the old;
Velvet hides an empty breast;
Satin's for the bold!

Lawn is for a bishop's yoke;
Linen's for a nun;
Satin is for wiser folk—
Would the dress were done!

Satin glows in candle-light—
Satin's for the proud!
They will say who watch at nighty
"What a fine shroud!"

Somebody's Song

This is what I vow;
 He shall have my heart to keep;
Sweetly will we stir and sleep.
  All the years, as now.
Swift the measured sands may run;
Love like this is never done;
He and I are welded one:
 This is what I vow.

 This is what I pray:
Keep him by me tenderly;
Keep him sweet in pride of me.
 Ever and a day;
Keep me from the old distress;
Let me, for our happiness.
Be the one to love the less:
 This is what I pray.

 This is what I know:
Lovers' oaths are thin as rain;
Love's a harbinger of pain—
 Would it were not so!
Ever is my heart a-thirst.
Ever is my love accurst;
He is neither last nor first—*
 This is what I know.

Anecdote

So silent I when Love was by
    He yawned, and turned away;
But Sorrow clings to my apron-strings^
    I have so much to say.

Braggart

The days will rally, wreathing
Their crazy tarantelle;
And you must go on breathing.
But I'll be safe in hell.

Like January weather,
The years will bite and smart.
And pull your bones together
To wrap your chattering heart.

The pretty stuff you're made of
Will crack and crease and dry.
The thing you are afraid of
Will look from every eye.

You will go faltering after
The bright, imperious line.
And split your throat on laughter.
And burn your eyes with brine.

You will be frail and musty
With peering, furtive head.
Whilst I am young and lusty.
Among the roaring dead.

Dorothy Parker

Epitaph for a Darling Lady

All her hours were yellow sands,
Blown in foolish whorls and tassels
Slipping warmly through her hands;
Patted into little castles.

Shiny day on shiny day
Tumble in a rainbow clutter,
As she flipped them all away.
Sent them spinning down the gutter.

Leave for her a red young rose.
Go your way, and save your pity;
She is happy, for she knows
That her dust is very pretty.

To a Much Too Unfortunate Lady

He will love you presently
If you be the way you be.
Send your heart a-skittering.
He will stoop, and lift the thing.
Be your dreams as thread, to tease
Into patterns he shall please.
Let him see your passion is
Ever tenderer than his. . . .
Go and bless your star above.
Thus are you, and thus is Love.

He will leave you white with woe.
If you go the way you go.
If your dreams were thread to weave^
He will pluck them from his sleeve.
If your heart had come to rest.
He will flick it from his breast.
Tender though the love he bore.
You had loved a little more. . . .
go and curse your star.
Thus Love is, and thus you are.

Paths

I SHALL tread, another year.
    Ways I walked with Grief,
Past the dry, ungarnered ear
    And the brittle leaf.

I shall stand, a year apart.
    Wondering, and shy,
Thinking, "Here she broke her heart;
    Here she pled to die."

I shall hear the pheasants call.
    And the raucous geese;
Down these ways, another Fall,
    I shall walk with Peace.

But the pretty path I trod
    Hand-in-hand with Love,—
Underfoot, the nascent sod.
    Brave young boughs above.

And the stripes of ribbon grass
    By the curling way,—
I shall never dare to pass
    To my dying day.

Hearthside

Half across the world from me
Lie the lands I'll never see—
I, whose longing lives and dies
Where a ship has sailed away;
I, that never close my eyes
But to look upon Cathay.

Things I may not know nor tell
Wait, where older waters swell;
Ways that flowered at Sappho's tread.
Winds that sighed in Homer's strings.
Vibrant with the singing dead.
Golden with the dust of wings.

Under deeper skies than mine.
Quiet valleys dip and shine.
Where their tender grasses heal
Ancient scars of trench and tomb
I shall never walk; nor kneel
Where the bones of poets bloom.

If I seek a lovelier part.
Where I travel goes my heart;
Where I stray my thought must go;
With me wanders my desire.
Best to sit and watch the snow,
Turn the lock, and poke the fire.

Dorothy Parker

The New Love

If it shine or if it rain,
    Little will I care or know.
Days, like drops upon a pane.
    Slip, and join, and go.

At my door's another lad;
    Here's his flower in my hair.
If he see me pale and sad.
    Will he see me fair?

I sit looking at the floor.
    Little will I think or say
If he seek another door;
    Even if he stay.

Rainy Night

Ghosts of all my lovely sins.
    Who attend too well my pillow.
Gay the wanton rain begins;
    Hide the limp and tearful willow.

Turn aside your eyes and ears,
    Trail away your robes of sorrow.
You shall have my further years,—
    You shall walk with me to-morrow.

I am sister to the rain;
    Fey and sudden and unholy.
Petulant at the windowpane.
    Quickly lost, remembered slowly.

I have lived with shades, a shade;
    I am hung with graveyard flowers.
Let me be to-night arrayed
    In the silver of the showers.

Every fragile thing shall rust;
    When another April passes
I may be a furry dust.
    Sifting through the brittle grasses.

All sweet sins shall be forgot
    Who will live to tell their siring?
Hear me now, nor let me rot
    Wistful still, and still aspiring.

Ghosts of dear temptations, heed;
    I am frail, be you forgiving.
See you not that I have need
    To be living with the living?

Sail, to-night, the Styx's breast;
    Glide among the dim processions
Of the exquisite unblest.
    Spirits of my shared transgressions.

Roam with young Persephone,
    Plucking poppies for your slumber . .
With the morrow, there shall be
    One more wraith among your number.

For a Sad Lady

And let her loves, when she is dead,
    Write this above her bones:
"No more she lives to give us bread
    Who asked her only stones."

Recurrence

We shall have our little day.
Take my hand and travel still
Round and round the little way,
Up and down the little hill.

It is good to love again;
Scan the renovated skies.
Dip and drive the idling pen.
Sweetly tint the paling lies.

Trace the dripping, piercèd heart.
Speak the fair, insistent verse.
Vow to God, and slip apart.
Little better, little worse.

Would we need not know before
How shall end this prettiness;
One of us must love the more.
One of us shall love the less.

Thus it is, and so it goes;
We shall have our day, my dear.
Where, unwilling, dies the rose
Buds the new, another year.

Story of Mrs. W—

M y garden blossoms pink and white^
    A place of decorous murmuring
Where I am safe from August night
    And cannot feel the knife of spring.

And I may walk the pretty place
    Before the curtsying hollyhocks
And laundered daisies, round of face—
    Good little girls, in party frocks.

My trees are amiably arrayed
    In pattern on the dappled sky.
And I may sit in filtered shade
    And watch the tidy years go by.

And I may amble pleasantly
    And hear my neighbors list their bones
And click my tongue in sympathy,
    And count the cracks in paving stones.

My door is grave in oaken strength.
    The cool of linen calms my bed.
And there at night I stretch my length
    And envy no one but the dead.

Dorothy Parker

The Dramatists

A STRING of shiny days we had,
    A spotless sky, a yellow sun;
And neither you nor I was sad
    When that was through and done.

But when, one day, a boy comes by
    And pleads me with your happiest vow,
"There was a lad I knew—I'll sigh;
    "I do not know him now."

And when another girl shall pass
    And speak a little name I said.
Then you will say "There was a lass—
    I wonder is she dead."

And each of us will sigh, and start
    A-talking of a faded year.
And lay a hand above a heart.
    And dry a pretty tear.

August

When my eyes are weeds.
And my lips are petals, spinning
Down the wind that has beginning
Where the crumpled beeches start
In a fringe of salty reeds;
When my arms are elder-bushes.
And the rangy lilac pushes
Upward, upward through my heart;

Summer, do your worst!
Light your tinsel moon, and call on
Your performing stars to fall on
Headlong through your paper sky;
Nevermore shall I be cursed
By a flushed and amorous slattern,
With her dusty laces' pattern
Trailing, as she straggles by.

The White Lady

I CANNOT rest, I cannot rest
    In strait and shiny wood,
My woven hands upon my breast—
    The dead are all so good!

The earth is cool across their eyes;
    They lie there quietly.
But I am neither old nor wise.
    They do not welcome me.

Where never I walked alone before
    I wander in the weeds;
And people scream and bar the door.
    And rattle at their beads.

We cannot rest, we never rest
    Within a narrow bed
Who still must love the living best—
    Who hate the drowsy dead!

I Know I Have Been Happiest

I know I have been happiest at your side;
But what is done, is done, and all's to be.
And small the good, to linger dolefully,—
Gaily it lived, and gallantly it died.
I will not make you songs of hearts denied.
And you, being man, would have no tears of me.
And should I offer you fidelity.
You'd be, I think, a little terrified.

Yet this the need of woman, this her curse:
To range her little gifts, and give, and give.
Because the throb of giving's sweet to bear.
To you, who never begged me vows or verse.
My gift shall be my absence, while I live;
But after that, my dear, I cannot swear.

Dorothy Parker

Testament

Oh, let it be a night of lyric rain
And singing breezes, when my bell is tolled.
I have so loved the rain that I would hold
Last in my ears its friendly, dim refrain.
I shall lie cool and quiet, who have lain
Fevered, and watched the book of day unfold.
Death will not see me flinch; the heart is bold
That pain has made incapable of pain.

Kinder the busy worms than ever love;
It will be peace to lie there, empty-eyed.
My bed made secret by the leveling showers.
My breast replenishing the weeds above.
And you will say of me, "Then has she died?
Perhaps I should have sent a spray of flowers."

"I Shall Come Back"

I shall come back without fanfaronade
Of wailing wind and graveyard panoply;
But, trembling, slip from cool Eternity—
A mild and most bewildered little shade.
I shall not make sepulchral midnight raid.
But softly come where I had longed to be
In April twilight's unsung melody,
And I, not you, shall be the one afraid.

Strange, that from lovely dreamings of the dead
I shall come back to you, who hurt me most.
You may not feel my hand upon your head.
I'll be so new and inexpert a ghost.
Perhaps you will not know that I am near,—
And that will break my ghostly heart, my dear.

Dorothy Parker

Condolence

They hurried here, as soon as you had died,
Their faces damp with haste and sympathy.
And pressed my hand in theirs, and smoothed my knee.
And clicked their tongues, and watched me, mournful-eyed.
Gently they told me of that Other Side—
How, even then, you waited there for me.
And what ecstatic meeting ours would be.
Moved by the lovely tale, they broke, and cried.

And when I smiled, they told me I was brave.
And they rejoiced that I was comforted.
And left, to tell of all the help they gave.
But I had smiled to think how you, the dead.
So curiously preoccupied and grave.
Would laugh, could you have heard the things they said.

The Immortals

If you should sail for Trebizond, or die,
Or cry another name in your first sleep,
Or see me board a train, and fail to sigh.
Appropriately, I'd clutch my breast and weep.
And you, if I should wander through the door.
Or sin, or seek a nunnery, or save
My lips and give my cheek, would tread the floor
And aptly mention poison and the grave.

Therefore the mooning world is gratified,
Quoting how prettily we sigh and swear;
And you and I, correctly side by side,
Shall live as lovers when our bones are bare;
And though we lie forever enemies.
Shall rank with Abélard and Heloise.

A Portrait

Because my love is quick to come and
A little here, and then a little there—
What use are any words of mine to swear
My heart is stubborn, and my spirit slow
Of weathering the drip and drive of woe?
What is my oath, when you have but to bare
My little, easy loves; and I can dare
Only to shrug, and answer, "They are so"

You do not know how heavy a heart it is
That hangs about my neck—a clumsy stone
Cut with a birth, a death, a bridal-day.
Each time I love, I find it still my own.
Who take it, now to that lad, now to this.
Seeking to give the wretched thing away.

PART TWO

Dorothy Parker

Portrait of the Artist

Oh, lead me to a quiet cell
    Where never footfall rankles
And bar the window passing well,
    And gyve my wrists and ankles.

Oh, wrap my eyes with linen fair.
    With hempen cord go bind me.
And, of your mercy, leave me there,
    Nor tell them where to find me.

Oh, lock the portal as you go.
    And see its holts be double. ...
Come back in half an hour or so.
    And I will be in trouble.

Chant for Dark Hours

Some men, some men
Cannot pass a
Book shop.
(Lady, make your mind up, and wait your life away.)

Some men, some men
Cannot pass a
Crap game.
(He said he'd come at moonrise, and here's another day!)

Some men, some men
Cannot pass a
Bar-room.
(Wait about, and hang about, and that's the way it goes.)

Some men, some men
Cannot pass a
Woman.
(Heaven never send me another one of those!)

Some men, some men
Cannot pass a
Golf course.
(Read a book, and sew a seam, and slumber if you can.)

Some men, some men
Cannot pass a
Haberdasher's.
(All your life you wait around for some damn man')

Dorothy Parker

Unfortunate Coincidence

B y the time you swear you're his,
    Shivering and sighing.
And he vows his passion is
    Infinite, undying—
Lady, make a note of this;
    One of you is lying.

Verse Reporting Late Arrival at a Conclusion

Consider a lady gone reckless in love.
    In novels and plays:
You watch her proceed in a drapery of
    A roseate haze.
Acclaimed as a riot, a wow, and a scream.
She flies with her beau to les Alpes Maritimes,
And moves in a mist of a mutual dream
    The rest of her days.

In life, if you'll listen to one who has been
    Observant of such,
A lady in love is more frequently in
    Decidedly Dutch.
The thorn, so to say, is revealed by the rose.
The best that she gets is a sock in the nose.
These authors and playwrights, I'm forced to suppose.
    Don't get around much,

Inventory

Four be the things I am wiser to know:
Idleness, sorrow, a friend, and a foe.

Four be the things I'd been better without:
Love, curiosity, freckles, and doubt.

Three be the things I shall never attain:
Envy, content, and sufficient champagne.

Three be the things I shall have till I dies
Laughter and hope and a sock in the eye.

Now at Liberty

Little white love, your way you've taken;
    Now I am left alone, alone.
Little white love, my heart's forsaken.
    (Whom shall I get by telephone?)
Well do I know there's no returning;
    Once you go out, it's done, it's done.
All of my days are gray with yearning.
    (Nevertheless, a girl needs fun.)

Little white love, perplexed and weary.
    Sadly your banner fluttered down.
Sullen the days, and dreary, dreary.
    (Which of the boys is still in town?)
Radiant and sure, you came a-flying;
    Puzzled, you left on lagging feet.
Slow in my breast, my heart is dying.
    (Nevertheless, a girl must eat.)

Little white love, I hailed you gladly;
    Now I must wave you out of sight.
Ah, but you used me badly, badly.
    (Who'd like to take me out to-night?)
All of the blundering words I've spoken.
    Little white love, forgive, forgive.
Once you went out, my heart fell, broken.
    (Nevertheless, a girl must live.)

Comment

Oh, life is a glorious cycle of song,
A medley of extemporanea;
And love is a thing that can never go wrong,
And I am Marie of Roumania.

Plea

Secrets, you said, would hold US two apart;
    You'd have me know of you your least transgression
And so the intimate places of your heart,
    Kneeling, you bared to me, as in confession.
Softly you told of loves that went before,—
    Of clinging arms, of kisses gladly given;
Luxuriously clean of heart once more.
    You rose up, then, and stood before me, shriven.

When this, my day of happiness, is through.
    And love, that bloomed so fair, turns brown and brittle.
There is a thing that I shall ask of you—
    I, who have given so much, and asked so little.
Some day, when there's another in my stead;
    Again you'll feel the need of absolution.
And you will go to her, and bow your head.
    And offer her your past, as contribution.

When with your list of loves you overcome her,
For Heaven's sake, keep this one secret from her!

Pattern

Leave me to my lonely pillow.
　　Go, and take your silly posies;
Who has vowed to wear the willow
　　Looks a fool, tricked out in roses.

Who are you, my lad, to ease me?
　　Leave your pretty words unspoken.
Tinkling echoes little please me.
　　Now my heart is freshly broken.

Over young are you to guide me.
　　And your blood is slow and sleeping.
If you must, then sit beside me. . . .
　　Tell me, why have I been weeping?

De Profundis

Oh, is it, then, Utopian
To hope that I may meet a man
Who'll not relate, in accents suave,
The tales of girls he used to have?

They Part

And if, my friend, you'd have it end,
    There's naught to hear or tell.
But need you try to black my eye
    In wishing me farewell?

Though I admit an edgèd wit
In woe is warranted.
May I be frank? . . . Such words as "-----"
Are better left unsaid.

There's rosemary for you and me;
    But is it usual, dear.
To hire a man, and fill a van
    By way of *souvenir*?

Ballade of a Great Weariness

There's little to have but the things I had,
    There's little to bear but the things I bore.
There's nothing to carry and naught to add.
    And glory to Heaven, I paid the score.

There's little to do hut I did before,
    There's little to learn but the things I know;
And this is the sum of a lasting lore:
    Scratch a lover, and find a foe.

And couldn't it be I was young and mad
    If ever my heart on my sleeve I wore?
There's many to claw at a heart unclad.
    And little the wonder it ripped and tore.
There's one that'll join in their push and roar.
    With stories to jabber, and stones to throw;
He'll fetch you a lesson that costs you sore—
    Scratch a lover, and find a foe.

So little I'll offer to you, my lad;
    It's little in loving I set my store.
There's many a maid would be flushed and glad.
    And better you'll knock at a kindlier door.
I'll dig at my lettuce, and sweep my floor—
    Forever, forever I'm done with woe—
And happen I'll whistle about my chore,
    "Scratch a lover and find a foe."

Dorothy Parker

L'ENVOI:

Oh, beggar or prince, no more, no more!
    Be off and away with your strut and show.
The sweeter the apple, the blacker the core—
    Scratch a lover, and find a foe!

Résumé

Razors pain you;
Rivers are damp;
Acids stain you;
And drugs cause cramp.
Guns aren't lawful;
Nooses give;
Gas smells awful;
You might as well live.

Dorothy Parker

Renunciation

Chloe's hair, no doubt, was brighter;
    Lydia's mouth more sweetly sad;
Hebe's arms were rather whiter;
    Languorous-lidded Helen had
Eyes more blue than e'er the sky was
Lalage's was subtler stuff;
Still, you used to think that I was
    Fair enough.

Now you're casting yearning glances
    At the pale Penelope;
Cutting in on Claudia's dances;
    Taking Iris out to tea.
Iole you find warm-hearted;
    Zoe's cheek is far from rough,—
Don't you think it's time we parted? ...
    Fair enough!

Day-Dreams

We'd build a little bungalow.
If you and I were one.
And carefully we'd plan it, so
We'd get the morning sun.
I'd rise each day at rosy dawn
And bustle gaily down;
In evening's cool, you'd spray the lawn
When you came back from town.

A little cook-book I should buy.
Your dishes I'd prepare;
And though they came out black and dry^
I know you wouldn't care.
How valiantly I'd strive to learn.
Assured you'd not complain!
And if my finger I should burn.
You'd kiss away the pain.

I'd buy a little scrubbing-brush
And beautify the floors;
I'd warble gaily as a thrush
About my little chores.
But though I'd cook and sew and scrub,
A higher life I'd find;
I'd join a little women's club
And cultivate my mind.

If you and I were one, my dear,
A model life we'd lead.
We'd travel on, from year to year.
At no increase of speed.

Ah, clear to me the vision of
The things that we should do!
And so I think it best, my love.
To string along as two.

The Veteran

When I was young and bold and strong.
Oh, right was right, and wrong was wrong
My plume on high, my flag unfurled,
I rode away to right the world.
"Come out, you dogs, and fight!" said I,
And wept there was but once to die.

But I am old; and good and bad
Are woven in a crazy plaid.
I sit and say, "The world is so;
And he is wise who lets it go.
A battle lost, a battle won—
The difference is small, my son."

Inertia rides and riddles me;
The which is called Philosophy.

Dorothy Parker

Prophetic Soul

Because your eyes are slant and slow.
    Because your hair is sweet to touch.
My heart is high again; but oh,
    I doubt if this will get me much.

Verse for a Certain Dog

Such glorious faith as fills your limpid eyes.
    Dear little friend of mine, I never knew.
All-innocent are you, and yet all-wise.
    (For heaven's sake, stop worrying that shoe!)
You look about, and all you see is fair;
    This mighty globe was made for you alone.
Of all the thunderous ages, you're the heir.
    (Get off the pillow with that dirty bone!)

A skeptic world you face with steady gaze;
    High in young pride you hold your noble head;
Gayly you meet the rush of roaring days.
    (*Must* you eat puppy biscuit on the bed?)
Lancelike your courage, gleaming swift and strong.
    Yours the white rapture of a winged soul.
Yours is a spirit like a May-day song.
    (God help you, if you break the goldfish bowl!)

"Whatever is, is good," your gracious creed.
    You wear your joy of living like a crown.
Love lights your simplest act, your every deed.
    (Drop it, I tell you—put that kitten down!)
You are God's kindliest gift of all,—a friend.
    Your shining loyalty unflecked by doubt.
You ask but leave to follow to the end.
    (Couldn't you wait until I took you out?)

Folk Tune

Other lads, their ways are daring;
 Other lads, they're not afraid;
Other lads, they show they're caring;
 Other lads—they know a maid.
Wiser Jock than ever you were.
 Will's with gayer spirit blest,
Robin's kindlier and truer,—
 Why should I love you the best?

Other lads, their eyes are bolder.
 Young they are, and strong and slim,
Ned is straight and broad of shoulder,
 Donald has a way with him.
David stands a head above you,
 Dick's as brave as Lancelot,—
Why, ah why, then, should I love you?
 Naturally, I do not.

Godspeed

Oh, seek, my love, your newer way
    I'll not be left in sorrow.
So long as I have yesterday.
    Go take your damned to-morrow!

Song of Perfect Propriety

I should like to ride the seas,
    A roaring buccaneer;
A cutlass banging at my knees,
    A dirk behind my ear.
And when my captives' chains would clank
    I'd howl with glee and drink.
And then fling out the quivering plank
    And watch the beggars sink.

I'd like to straddle gory decks.
    And dig in laden sands.
And know the feel of throbbing necks
    Between my knotted hands.

Oh, I should like to strut and curse
    Among my blackguard crew. . . .
But I am writing little verse,
    As little ladies do.

Oh, I should like to dance and laugh
    And pose and preen and sway.
And rip the hearts of men in half.
    And toss the bits away.

I'd like to view the reeling years
    Through unastonished eyes.
And dip my finger-tips in tears.
    And give my smiles for sighs.

I'd stroll beyond the ancient bounds,
    And tap at fastened gates.
And hear the prettiest of sounds,—
    The clink of shattered fates.

My slaves I'd like to bind with thongs
    That cut and burn and chill. . .
But I am writing little songs,
    As little ladies will,

Dorothy Parker

Social Note

Lady, lady, should you meet
One whose ways are all discreet.
One who murmurs that his wife
Is the lodestar of his life.
One who keeps assuring you
That he never was untrue.
Never loved another one . . .
Lady, lady, better run!

One Perfect Rose

A single flow'r he sent me, since we met.
    All tenderly his messenger he chose;
Deep-hearted, pure, with scented dew still wet—
    One perfect rose.

I knew the language of the floweret;
    "My fragile leaves,'' it said, "his heart enclose."
Love long has taken for his amulet
    One perfect rose.

Why is it no one ever sent me yet
    One perfect limousine, do you suppose?
Ah no, it's always just my luck to get
    One perfect rose.

Ballade at Thirty-five

This, no song of an ingenue,
　　This, no ballad of innocence;
This, the rhyme of a lady who
　　Followed ever her natural bents.

This, a solo of sapience.
　　This, a chantey of sophistry.
This, the sum of experiments,—
　　I loved them until they loved me.

Decked in garments of sable hue.
　　Daubed with ashes of myriad Lents,
Wearing shower bouquets of rue.
　　Walk I ever in penitence.

Oft I roam, as my heart repents.
　　Through God's acre of memory.
Marking stones, in my reverence,
　　"I loved them until they loved me."

Pictures pass me in long review,—
　　Marching columns of dead events.
I was tender, and, often, true;
　　Ever a prey to coincidence.

Always knew I the consequence;
　　Always saw what the end would be.
We're as Nature has made us—hence
　　I loved them until they loved me.

L'ENVOI:

Princes, never I'd give offense.
    Won't you think of me tenderly?
Here's my strength and my weakness, gents,
    I loved them until they loved me.

Dorothy Parker

The Thin Edge

With you, my heart is quiet here.
And all my thoughts are cool as rain.
I sit and let the shifting year
Go by before the window-pane.
And reach my hand to yours, my dear . . .
I wonder what it's like in Spain.

Spring Song

(in the expected manner)

Enter Aprils laughingly.
    Blossoms in her tumbled hair.
High of heart, and fancy-free—
    When was maiden half so fair?
Bright her eyes with easy tears.
    Wanton-sweet, her smiles for men.
"Winter's gone," she cries, "and here's
    Spring again."

When we loved, 'twas April, too;
    Madcap April—urged us on.
Just as she did, so did you—
    Sighed, and smiled, and then were gone.
How she plied her pretty arts.
    How she laughed and sparkled then!
April, make love in our hearts
    Spring again!

Love Song

My own dear love, he is strong and bold
    And he cares not what comes after.
His words ring sweet as a chime of gold.
    And his eyes are lit with laughter.
He is jubilant as a flag unfurled—
    Oh, a girl, she'd not forget him.
My own dear love, he is all my world,—
    And I wish I'd never met him.

My love, he's mad, and my love, he's fleet.
    And a wild young wood-thing bore him!
The ways are fair to his roaming feet.
    And the skies are sunlit for him.
As sharply sweet to my heart he seems
    As the fragrance of acacia.
My own dear love, he is all my dreams,—
    And I wish he were in Asia.

My love runs by like a day in June,
    And he makes no friends of sorrows.
He'll tread his galloping rigadoon
    In the pathway of the morrows.
He'll live his days where the sunbeams start.
    Nor could storm or wind uproot him.
My own dear love, he is all my heart,—
    And I wish somebody'd shoot him.

Indian Summer

In youth, it was a way I had
    To do my best to please.
And change, with every passing lad.
    To suit his theories.

But now I know the things I know.
    And do the things I do;
And if you do not like me so.
    To hell, my love, with you!

Dorothy Parker

Philosophy

If I should labor through daylight and dark.
Consecrate, valorous, serious, true.
Then on the world I may blazon my mark;
And what if I don't, and what if I do?

For an Unknown Lady

Lady, if you'd slumber sound,
Keep your eyes upon the ground.
If you'd toss and turn at night.
Slip your glances left and right.
Would the mornings find you gay.
Never give your heart away.
Would they find you pale and sad.
Fling it to a whistling lad.
Ah, but when his pleadings burn.
Will you let my words return?
Will you lock your pretty lips.
And deny your finger-tips.
Veil away your tender eyes.
Just because some words were wise?
If he whistles low and clear
When the insistent moon is near
And the secret stars are known,—
Will your heart be still your own
Just because some words were true? . . .
Lady, I was told them, too!

Dorothy Parker

The Leal

The friends I made have slipped and strayed,
    And who's the one that cares?
A trifling lot and best forgot—
    And that's my tale, and theirs.

Then if my friendships break and bend.
    There's little need to cry
The while I know that every foe
    Is faithful till I die.

Finis

Now it's over, and now it's done;
    Why does everything look the same?
Just as bright, the unheeding sun,—
    Can't it see that the parting came?
People hurry and work and swear.
    Laugh and grumble and die and wed,
Ponder what they will eat and wear,—
    Don't they know that our love is dead?

Just as busy, the crowded street;
    Cars and wagons go rolling on.
Children chuckle, and lovers meet,—
    Don't they know that our love is gone?
No one pauses to pay a tear;
    None walks slow, for the love that's through,—
I might mention, my recent dear,
    I've reverted to normal, too.

Dorothy Parker

Words of Comfort to he Scratched on a Mirror

Helen of Troy had a wandering glance;
A Sappho's restriction was only the sky;
Ninon was ever the chatter of France;   `
But oh, what a good girl am I!

Men

They hail you as their morning star
Because you are the way you are.
If you return the sentiment,
They'll try to make you different;
And once they have you, safe and sound.
They want to change you all around.
Your moods and ways they put a curse on;
They'd make of you another person.
They cannot let you go your gait;
They influence and educate.
They'd alter all that they admired.
They make me sick, they make me tired.

News Item

Men seldom make passes
At girls who wear glasses.

Song of One of the Girls

Here in my heart I am Helen;
    I'm Aspasia and Hero, at least.
I'm Judith, and Jael, and Madame de Staël;
I'm Salome, moon of the East.

Here in my soul I am Sappho;
    Lady Hamilton am I, as well.
In me Récamier vies with Kitty O'Shea,
With Dido, and Eve, and poor Nell.

I'm of the glamorous ladies
    At whose beckoning history shook.
But you are a man, and see only my pan.
    So I stay at home with a book.

Lullaby

Sleep, pretty lady, the night is enfolding you,
 Drift, and so lightly, on crystalline streams.
Wrapped in its perfumes, the darkness is holding you;
 Starlight bespangles the way of your dreams.
Chorus the nightingales, wistfully amorous;
 Blessedly quiet, the blare of the day.
All the sweet hours may your visions be glamorous,—
 Sleep, pretty lady, as long as you may.

Sleep, pretty lady, the night shall be still for you;
 Silvered and silent, it watches your rest.
Each little breeze, in its eagerness, will for you
 Murmur the melodies ancient and blest.
So in the midnight does happiness capture us;
 Morning is dim with another day's tears.
Give yourself sweetly to images rapturous,—
 Sleep, pretty lady, a couple of years.

Sleep, pretty lady, the world awaits day with you;
 Girlish and golden, the slender young moon.
Grant the fond darkness its mystical way with you,
 Morning returns to us ever too soon.
Roses unfold, in their loveliness, all for you;
 Blossom the lilies for hope of your glance.
When you're awake, all the men go and fall for you,—
 Sleep, pretty lady, and give me a chance.

Faut de Mieux

Travel, trouble, music, art,
    A kiss, a frock, a rhyme,—
I never said they feed my heart.
    But still they pass my time.

Dorothy Parker

Roundel

She's passing fair; but so demure is she
   So quiet is her gown, so smooth her hair,
That few there are who note her and agree
   She's passing fair.

Yet when was ever beauty held more rare
Than simple heart and maiden modesty?
What fostered charms with virtue could compare

Alas, no lover ever stops to see;
The best that she is offered is the air.
Yet—if the passing mark is minus
      D—
   She's passing fair.

A Certain Lady

Oh, I can smile for you, and tilt my head.
　　And drink your rushing words with eager lips.
And paint my mouth for you a fragrant red.
　　And trace your brows with tutored finger-tips.
When you rehearse your list of loves to me.
　　Oh, I can laugh and marvel, rapturous-eyed.
And you laugh back, nor can you ever see
　　The thousand little deaths my heart has died.
And you believe, so well I know my part.
　　That I am gay as morning, light as snow.
And all the straining things within my heart
　　You'll never know.

Oh, I can laugh and listen, when we meet.
　　And you bring tales of fresh adventurings,—
Of ladies delicately indiscreet.
　　Of lingering hands, and gently whispered things.
And you are pleased with me, and strive anew
　　To sing me sagas of your late delights.
Thus do you want me—marveling, gay, and true.
　　Nor do you see my staring eyes of nights.
And when, in search of novelty, you stray.
　　Oh, I can kiss you blithely as you go. . . .
And what goes on, my love, while you're away.
　　You'll never know.

Observation

If I don't drive around the park,
I'm pretty sure to make my mark.
If I'm in bed each night by ten,
I may get back my looks again.
If I abstain from fun and such.
I'll probably amount to much.
But I shall stay the way I am.
Because I do not give a damn.

Symptom Recital

I do not like my state of mind;
I'm bitter, querulous, unkind.
I hate my legs, I hate my hands,
I do not yearn for lovelier lands.
I dread the dawn's recurrent light;
I hate to go to bed at night.
I snoot at simple, earnest folk.
I cannot take the gentlest joke.
I find no peace in paint or type.
My world is but a lot of tripe.
I'm disillusioned, empty-breasted.
For what I think, I'd be arrested,
I am not sick, I am not well.
My quondam dreams are shot to hell.
My soul is crushed, my spirit sore;
I do not like me any more.
I cavil, quarrel, grumble, grouse.
I ponder on the narrow house.
I shudder at the thought of men. . .
I'm due to fall in love again.

Fighting Words

Say my love is easy had.
  Say I'm bitten raw with pride,
Sav I am too often sad,—
  Still behold me at your side.

Say I'm neither brave nor young.
  Say I woo and coddle care.
Say the devil touched my tongue,—
  Still you have my heart to wear.

But say my verses do not scan.
  And I get me another man!

Rondeau Redouble

(and scarcely worth the trouble, at that)

The same to me are sombre days and gay.
    Though joyous dawns the rosy morn, and bright.
Because my dearest love is gone away
    Within my heart is melancholy night.

My heart beats low in loneliness, despite
    That riotous Summer holds the earth in sway.
In cerements my spirit is bedight;
    The same to me are sombre days and gay.

Though breezes in the rippling grasses play,
    And waves dash high and far in glorious might,
I thrill no longer to the sparkling day.
    Though joyous dawns the rosy morn, and bright.

Ungraceful seems to me the swallow's flight;
    As well might Heaven's blue be sullen gray;
My soul discerns no beauty in their sight
    Because my dearest love is gone away.

Let roses fling afar their crimson spray.
    And virgin daisies splash the fields with white.
Let bloom the poppy hotly as it may.
    Within my heart is melancholy night.

And this, oh love, my pitiable plight
    Whenever from my circling arms you stray;
This little world of mine has lost its light. . . .
    I hope to God, my dear, that you can say
                The same to me.

Dorothy Parker

Autobiography

Oh, both my shoes are shiny new.
    And pristine is my hat;
My dress is 1922. . . .
    My life is all like that.

The Choice

He'd have given me rolling lands,
    Houses of marble, and billowing farms,
Pearls, to trickle between my hands.
    Smoldering rubies, to circle my arms.

You you'd only a lilting song.
    Only a melody, happy and high.
You were sudden and swift and strong,—
    Never a thought for another had I.

He'd have given me laces rare.
    Dresses that glimmered with frosty sheen.
Shining ribbons to wrap my hair.
    Horses to draw me, as fine as a queen.

You—you'd only to whistle low.
    Gaily I followed wherever you led.
I took you, and I let him go,—
    Somebody ought to examine my head!

Ballade of Big Plans

> She loved him. He knew it.
> And love was a game that two could play at.
> —"Julia Cane," p. 280.

Once the orioles sang in chorus.
Once the skies were a cloudless blue.
Spring bore blossoms expressly for us.
Stars lined up to spell "Y-O-U."
All the world wore a golden hue.
Life was a thing to be bold and gay at;
Love was the only game I knew.
And love is a game that two can play at.

Now the heavens are scowling o'er us.
Now the blossoms are pale and few.
Love was a rose with thorns that tore us.
Love was a ship without a crew.
Love is untender, and love is untrue.
Love is a moon for a dog to bay at.
Love is the Lady-That's-Known-as-Lou,
And love is a game that two can play at.

Recollections can only bore us;
Now it's over, and now it's through.
Our day is dead as a dinosaurus.
Other the paths that you pursue.
What is the girl in the case to do?
What is she going to spend her day at?
Fun demands, at a minimum, two—
And love is a game that two can play at.

L'ENVOI:

Prince, I'm packing away the rue.
I'll give them something to shout "Hooray"
I've got somebody else in view:
And love is a game that two can play at.

Dorothy Parker

General Review of the Sex Situation

Woman wants monogamy;
Man delights in novelty.
Love is woman's moon and sun;
Man has other forms of fun.
Woman lives but in her lord;
Count to ten, and man is bored.
With this the gist and sum of it,
What earthly good can come of it?

Inscription for the Ceiling of a Bedroom

Daily dawns another day;
I must up, to make my way.
Though I dress and drink and eat.
Move my fingers and my feet.
Learn a little, here and there.
Weep and laugh and sweat and swear.
Hear a song, or watch a stage.
Leave some words upon a page.
Claim a foe, or hail a friend—
Bed awaits me at the end.

Though I go in pride and strength.
I'll come back to bed at length.
Though I walk in blinded woe,
Back to bed I'm bound to go.
High my heart, or bowed my head.
All my days but lead to bed.
Up, and out, and on; and then
Ever back to bed again.
Summer, Winter, Spring, and Fall—
I'm a fool to rise at all!

Dorothy Parker

Pictures in the Smoke

Oh, gallant was the first love, and glittering and fine;
    The second love was water, in a clear white cup;
The third love was his, and the fourth was mine;
    And after that, I always get them all mixed up.

Biographies

1

Now this is the story of Lucy Brown,
A glittering jewel in virtue's crown.
From earliest youth, she aspired to please.
She never fell down and dirtied her knees;
She put all her pennies in savings banks;
She never omitted her "please" and "thanks";
She swallowed her spinach without a squawk;
And patiently listened to Teacher's talk;
She thoughtfully stepped over worms and ants;
And earnestly watered the potted plants;
She didn't dismember expensive toys;
And never would play with the little boys.

And when to young womanhood Lucy came
Her mode of behavior was just the same.
She always was safe in her home at dark;
And never went riding around the park;
She wouldn't put powder upon her nose;
And petticoats sheltered her spotless hose;
She knew how to market and mend and sweep;
By quarter-past ten, she was sound asleep;
In presence of elders, she held her tongue—
The way that they did when the world was young.
And people remarked, in benign accord,
"You'll see that she gathers her just reward."

Observe, their predictions were more than fair.
She married an affluent millionaire
So gallant and handsome and wise and gay.

And rated in Bradstreet at Double A.
And she lived with him happily all her life,
And made him a perfectly elegant wife.

2

Now Marigold Jones, from her babyhood.
Was bad as the model Miss Brown was good.
She stuck out her tongue at her grieving nurse;
She frequently rifled her Grandma's purse;
She banged on the table and broke the plates;
She jeered at the passing inebriates;
And tore all her dresses and ripped her socks;
And shattered the windows with fair-sized rocks;
The words on the fences she'd memorize;
She blackened her dear little brother's eyes;
And cut off her sister's abundant curls;
And never would play with the little girls.

And when she grew up—as is hardly strange—
Her manner of life underwent no change
But faithfully followed her childhood plan.
And once there was talk of a married man!
She sauntered in public in draperies
Affording no secrecy to her knees;
She constantly uttered what was not true;
She flirted and petted, or what have you;
And, tendered advice by her kind Mamma,
Her answer, I shudder to state, was "Blah!"
And people remarked, in sepulchral tones,
"You'll see what becomes of Marigold Jones."

Observe, their predictions were more than fair.
She married an affluent millionaire
So gallant and handsome and wise and gay.
And rated in Bradstreet at Double A.
And she lived with him happily all her life.
And made him a perfectly elegant wife.

Nocturne

Always I knew that it could not last
    (Gathering clouds, and the snowflakes flying).
Now it is part of the golden past;
    (Darkening skies, and the night-wind sighing)
It is but cowardice to pretend.
    Cover with ashes our love's cold crater,—
Always I've known that it had to end
    Sooner or later.

Always I knew it would come like this
    (Pattering rain, and the grasses springing).
Sweeter to you is a new love's kiss
    (Flickering sunshine, and young birds singing).
Gone are the raptures that once we knew.
    Now you are finding a new joy greater,—
Well, I'll be doing the same thing, too.
    Sooner or later.

Interview

The ladies men admire, I've heard.
Would shudder at a wicked word.
Their candle gives a single light;
They'd rather stay at home at night.
They do not keep awake till three.
Nor read erotic poetry.
They never sanction the impure.
Nor recognize an overture.
They shrink from powders and from paints . . .
So far, I've had no complaints.

Song in a Minor Key

There's a place I know where the birds swing low.
    And wayward vines go roaming.
Where the lilacs nod, and a marble god
    Is pale, in scented gloaming.
And at sunset there comes a lady fair
    Whose eyes are deep with yearning.
By an old, old gate does the lady wait
    Her own true love's returning.

But the days go by, and the lilacs die.
    And trembling birds seek cover;
Yet the lady stands, with her long white hands
    Held out to greet her lover.
And it's there she'll stay till the shadowy day
    A monument they grave her.
She will always wait by the same old gate,—
    The gate her true love gave her.

Experience

Some men break your heart in two.
   Some men fawn and flatter.
Some men never look at you;
   And that cleans up the matter.

Dorothy Parker

Neither Bloody Nor Bowed

They say of me, and so they should,
It's doubtful if I come to good.
I see acquaintances and friends
Accumulating dividends.
And making enviable names
In science, art, and parlor games.
But I, despite expert advice.
Keep doing things I think are nice.
And though to good I never come—
Inseparable my nose and thumb!

The Burned Child

Love has had his way with me.
    This my heart is torn and maimed
Since he took his play with me.
    Cruel well the bow-boy aimed.

Shot, and saw the feathered shaft
    Dripping bright and bitter red.
He that shrugged his wings and laughed—
    Better had he left me dead.

Sweet, why do you plead me, then.
    Who have bled so sore of that?
Could I bear it once again? . . .
    Drop a hat, dear, drop a hat!

Summary

Dorothy Parker was a force like no other, in a world which was primarily male. She plowed straight through the 'boy's club' atmosphere and made her mark. She deserves immense respect for her trail-blazing actions!

It's inspiring to see what she was able to accomplish.

I'd love to hear your thoughts on this book!

Thank you for reading *Enough Rope*!

If you enjoyed this presentation, please leave feedback. All of my (Lisa Shea)'s proceeds from this book benefit local arts programs. Together we can help make a difference!

Be sure to sign up for my free newsletter! You'll get alerts of free books, discounts, and new releases. I run my own newsletter server – nobody else will ever see your email address. I promise!

http://www.lisashea.com/lisabase/subscribe.html

Please visit the following pages for news about free books, discounted releases, and new launches. Feel free to post questions there – I strive to answer within a day!

Facebook:

https://www.facebook.com/LisaSheaAuthor

Twitter:

https://twitter.com/LisaSheaAuthor

Blog:

http://www.lisashea.com/lisabase/blog/

Share the news – we all want to enjoy interesting novels!

Dedication

To the Sutton Writing Group and Boston Writer's Group, which support me in all my writing quests.

Most of all, to my loyal fans who support me on Goodreads, Facebook, Twitter, and other platforms. It's because of you that I keep writing!

About the Editor

I've been writing poetry and creating art since I was quite young. I've published over 450 books in a variety of fiction and non-fiction genres.

Namaste.

Free Ebooks

All of the following ebooks should be available free on all platforms.

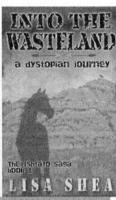

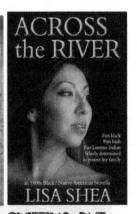

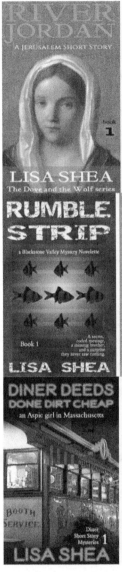

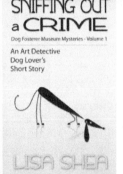

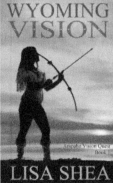

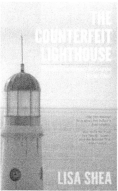

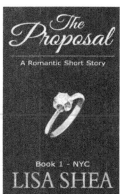

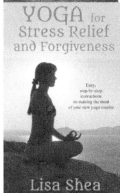

I may have added more free books since releasing this list here. For the most up to date version, be sure to visit:

http://www.lisashea.com/freebooks/

Thank you for supporting the cause!

Be the change you wish to see in the world.

Made in the USA
Las Vegas, NV
22 March 2023

69508820R00073